MY TALK BO

I am in the darkness and the light
I see things but many things elude me
I am night and day
Physical and spiritual
Earthly

Many thoughts have I
Regrets
But in all I do, I have truth
My truth that stays with me

Michelle Jean

Wow is all I can say after finishing book nine in the My Talk Book Series.

Yesterday (June 04, 2015) dreamt I was home in Jamaica, my little area in Clarendon where I grew up. I don't know what happened but Lady Saw (Marion Hall) was there. She purchased a house and the people she bought the house from scammed her. She did not own the house. She wanted to go after the people legally and I said I would help her. I don't know why I am dreaming about her because I had voiced my displeasure of her in one of my book blogs.

Do I know what this dream means?

Yes because this dream pertains to me and or my family as well. Like I've said and will say again, I will not fight anyone fi dead lef.

If you want to cheat me out of what is rightfully mine, then go right ahead because I know the God I look to for everything. Today a fi yu but tomorrow is a whole different story. Hence I claim tomorrow and tomorrow is infinitely and indefinitely mine.

__And no people it's not my family that is cheating me; my family is being cheated.__ Hence I leave wicked and evil people to time and their wickedness. I know the destruction of man and the *death of man, so I worry not about wicked and evil people. Evil has time and the time of evil has and have come to an end. I am just waiting for physical time to catch up to that point in time (spiritual time at that moment in time) for all to be over.*

I know time hence spiritual time is further ahead in time. Therefore, physical time and spiritual time are not on the same accord.

Like I said, evil hath time because evil hath an end, but life, true life hath no end.

Yes the dreams are weird because I am on the white level again and it seems like I can't come off it.

Dreamt this morning (June 05, 2015) about Satan and Death. Man oh man have I opened up the pathway for every wicked and evil nation to come after me. Hence the can of whoop ass has and have been opened by me but I worry not about this.

Thus my dream world was all about Satan and his band of trolls of worse than demons coming after me.

Dreamt Jay-Z and Beyonce coming after me. Here I escaped them via escalators that went up not down. In this dream I was surrounded by people; men of the South Pacific as well as Chinese people (females and males). I kept going into their business place; stores. In one particular store (Chinese store) this lady; owner had grapes of different kinds along with other produce. One particular kind of grape was illegal for her to sell so I could not get it to buy. I remember tasting one grape and it was sweet but when she gave me and or showed me grapes of a different bunch and I tasted one, it was sour. When I cringed this Chinese Man said, some of the grapes are sour at this time of the year. Soh as ole people sey, we sweet yu, a goh sowa yu. Now I am thinking about what I said about Germany in book nine and other nations. But you know what people; I care not what any race have to say. Like I said, I have a job to do and I am doing it to the best of my ability. I cannot concern myself about wicked and evil people and countries.

As humans we do not respect each other nor each other's values and home; country. We fight and kill amongst each other and expect Good God and Allelujah; Lovey to just turn the other cheek and he cannot do that.

Many things hurt me and I voice them. I take my concerns and anger to Lovey and Good God and I tell him of my pain and hurt. I refuse to be a hypocrite when it comes to my feelings. We cannot say we love and do all manner of vile things towards others. I would rather walk away from Lovey than save people that truly hurt me and my people, whoever those people are.

Why the hell should I save you when you have no respect for me, my people, my country and True Love, Good God and Allelujah?

Bleep you and chuck. I don't like you for what you did hence truly do not look to me to save you because I will not. Like I said, I would rather walk away from Lovey and spit on the ground rather than save you.

If you hate me, don't pretend to like me.

If you can't stand me don't come near me nor come and live near me.

If you hate me, don't come to my funeral and pretend to like me. Sey di bitch dead but don't pretend.

If you hate me, don't even come to my funeral because the day you do, is the day you will be lifted up off the ground by my spirit and tossed the hell far away from my grave site. I will tumble you down, so don't come around my resting place. And people don't say this cannot be done, it can and will be done. If I don't like you, I truly don't like you and I will not harbour you around me.

You are to love everyone and this is the godly thing to do. And I say unto you, bleep you infinitely and indefinitely because we are not all Good God's children. Billions of humans Lovey truly do not know, so don't tell me about we are all God's and or Good God and Lovey's children. When you say this you are overstepping your boundaries. You are telling Lovey that the devil's children and or seed is his also.

You can't tell him that but I can when I am angry at him. And yes when I want to truly piss him off so that he can feel my hurt and pain.

You did not make him Lovey your beating stick and All, I did. So you cannot pass your place or pass judgment when it comes to him.

Evil is evil and evil cannot be good period.

Many of you get involved in the occult and don't even know which side you are on when it comes to Sin and or the Devil and or Satan.

666 damn I love this number.

Oh my God I can't believe you said that you are saying with your hand (s) to your mouth.

666 is time; female death. Yes the three (3) daughters (triplets) that Satan had with Eve. You know them as Cain, Abel and Seth but in their original form they are three gorgeous bi-racial girls. They walk in unison and each one of them has a 6 in their forehead. And yes they are in black. Beautiful girls, very beautiful. So when you as occultist pledge allegiance to Satan and use 666, you are pledging allegiance to female death not male death hence your five (5) pointed star and not 6 (six) pointed star. And yes, you are pledging allegiance to ***BLACK DEATH AND NOT WHITE DEATH.*** Know the truth come on now.

When you use 6666 you are referring to Satan Himself; Male Death. Hence your six pointed star and Mogen and or Megan David and or Star of David. And besides I did tell you this in some of my other books in the Michelle Jean Series of Books.

Yes I told you about Jay-Z and Beyonce in some of my Book Blogs. So nothing is new to me in what I see when it comes to the devil and his band of trolls trying to kill me.

Listen people, the set up is there.
The anguish is going to be there but it makes no sense anymore. Death is coming for humanity. There is no escaping this for billions because guess what, we as humans gave death a home due to our sins. We were told specifically not to do certain things and we did them anyway.

We showed Lovey disrespect in all that we do. We disrespected him and now that he's stepped aside from us, we are saying we're confused and don't know what to do.

We as humans were the ones to believe in sacrifices.

We as humans were the ones to believe in all manner of evil.

We as humans were the ones to sell our souls to the devil as you call him.

We as humans were the ones to give our lives over to death.

We as humans were the ones to kill for a place in hell.

We as humans were the ones to listen to religious leaders tell us lies about heaven and hell including tell us lies about Lovey and how he sacrificed his son to save your wicked and evil asses.

You sinned reckless and rude and Lovey is to put up his child as a ransom to save your wretched souls. Please, Lovey a nuh puppu nennay come on now. Sin not and live. Lovey is not your scapegoat or sacrificial lamb for any of you and neither is his good and true people. Clean your damned selves up and live come on now. Damn wrenk. Why the hell should someone die to save you?

Your sins are not my sins, so why should anyone be responsible for them? You made the decision to sin so take care of your own mess come on now. Who the hell are you for someone to die; lose their soul over and or for? Listen nuh mek mi get mad. Damn outtaada. Who yu? Yu life nuh worth more than mine so quibba yu stinking self.

Yes my dream world was filled with evil people. Dreamt Satan like I said, but this time he was not handsome. He was a monster with fire around him. He came after me but failed to kill me. He was consumed in his own fire; the fire of hell.

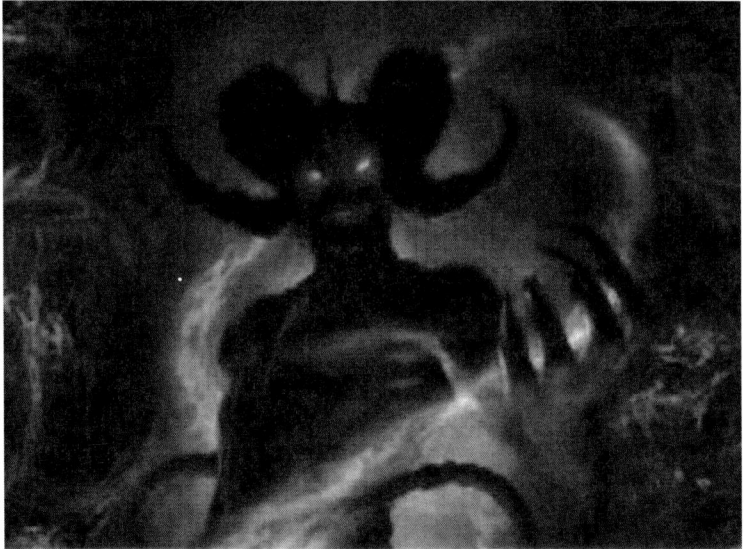

Picture taken from the internet and no copyright infringement intended. This is not the exact picture in my dream. Satan's horns were pointy and he did not have a tail nor was his hand like that, but you get the idea of what I was up against in my dream. There was more fire. The picture I saw reminded me of a movie hence everyone in my dream was and or were American Entertainers.

So this Satan as in the picture above failed, was consumed by his own fire like I said.

Also dreamt about Rosemary's Baby, Mia Farrow and how death was after me; tried to kill me yet again but failed. Death ended up dying in this dream and or vision as well.

Dreamt Drew Barrymore and this other young lady was in bed. This had to do with death also but death failed. In the end, Drew was eating a freeze and so was the young lady beside her. Drew took a piece of her mango, no not mango, but that funny looking freeze you get in the package that no one really wants. She spat the freeze at me from a distance. It wasn't in a spitting gesture to be rude but to share like how you would share with your partner if you share simple intimacy like this with him or her. Suffice it to say, I did not partake in the freeze but a sweet taste was left in my mouth.

So all my dreams this morning (June 05, 2015) had to do with death coming after me like I've said. Yes I've rubbed a lot of people the wrong way but like I said, it matters not anymore. Death is coming to earth and there isn't a damned thing billions can do to save self. Some of you did sign a contract with death and they have to abide by this deadly contract.

We know not about life and death. Yes we have a choice and billions did choose death over life. See billions of you were banking on the sacrifice of one individual to save you, ***but in all you've been taught, everyone forgot that HE GOOD***

GOD AND ALLELUJUAH WILL NEVER EVER SACRIFICE HIS OWN TO SAVE THE WICKED AND EVIL OF ANY LAND OR HOME.

Life cannot sacrifice life because life is not death, death is death and when you give yourself over to death, you are going to die.

As humans we knew the deceit of evil's children but yet we trust these wicked and evil people to guide us on the right path. How can liars and thieves guide correctly come on now?

If all a man knows is lies, will he not tell them; tell these lies to you?

If a man was brought up to steal, will he not steal from you also?

So in all we as humans know, we know lies and not the truth. Hence we tell lies and live by these lies without knowing that these lies and the lies that you tell, kill you; take you straight to hell.

So yes evil will seek to kill me but I leave my fate and good and true life in the hands of Lovey, Good God and Allelujah.

Like I said, I am not here to interfere with the devil's children and people because their end is near. Every man woman and child must pay according to his or her own works.

All who are evil, their name is written in the book of Judges due to sin. So I truly worry not about them. I have my good and clean life that I have to live and I refuse to be hypocritical about life and death. I know the truth; hence it's the truth that I must live for and by.

NO ONE WANTS TO GO TO HELL, BUT YET WE SIN AND OR CONTINUE SINNING TO GET THERE AND I TRY DO NOT KNOW WHY. You know hell is bad for you, why do all to get and or go there? Save yourself come on now.

If you want good for yourself then do good. Yes it's hard to walk on the pathway of goodness and truth; righteousness because there are wicked and evil people and spirits there to throw you off. But if humanity wanted to live and or needed goodness for self, then the laws that were set out by Lovey for us via his messengers *WE WOULD HAVE KEPT. WE WOULD NOT BREAK THEM SO WILLINGLY.*

We all know the *"WAGES OF SIN IS DEATH,"* but yet we sin anyway. We do not think of the consequences that are associated with sin. *24000 years death had to make humanity fall and death and or sin did their job. Humanity did fall because we sinned reckless and rude. Death and or sin won over man and there's not a damned thing we can do about it to save ourselves. The planet of death is on earth because I saw it and I told you about it in book nine. We cannot stop death because we as humans made death unstoppable with our sins come on now.*

We hate each other based on hue.

Lands and or nations fight against nations because they cannot get along. So brother fight against brother without knowing what they are fighting for.

Instead of lifting the curse, we sink ourselves further in the curse for what?

Go back to SURVIVOR by Bugle and hear what he said about mankind and religion. He said, don't tell him about religion because it's a divider and he is infinitely and indefinitely correct. *Religion do not bring nations together, religion separate them and cause us to hate each other.*

Religion is about dominance and control.

Religion pit this god against this god and so forth.

RELIGION IS WAR; DEATH, hence religion and or death have a great impact in and on our lives.

We take what these people tell us at face value without looking into things by going to Lovey, Good God and Allelujah directly.

IF THE RELIGIONS OF EARTH; MAN WAS SO HOLY, WHY ARE PEDOPHILES IN THEM?

IF THE RELIGIONS OF EARTH; MAN WAS SO HOLY, WHY DO THEY PRESIDE OVER DEATH?

IF THE RELIGIONS OF EARTH; MAN WAS SO HOLY, WHY ARE THEY NOT UNIFIED WITH EACH OTHER?

MORE IMPORTANTLY, WHY ARE THEY NOT UNIFIED WITH LOVEY, GOOD GOD AND ALLELUJAH?

IF THE RELIGIONS OF EARTH; MAN WAS SO HOLY, WHY DO THEY TAKE AWAY FROM THE LIFE OF MAN AND GOOD GOD?

IF THE RELIGIONS OF EARTH; MAN WAS SO HOLY, WHY DO THEY NOT TEACH AND PREACH FROM THE SAME HOLY BOOK?

IF THE RELIGIONS OF EARTH; MAN WAS SO HOLY, WHY IS MAN SLATED TO DIE BEFORE 2032?

Hence as humans we do not think of the impact lies and or religious lies play in our lives. We do not put Good God and Allelujah first in all that we do. We would rather listen to the lies of these religious fanatics rather than listen to the good voice of Good God and Allelujah; Lovey.

And yes you can say I am a religious fanatic. Go ahead say it so I can blast you and cuss you good and proper. Yes I defend Lovey and will forever defend him because there is only so much he can do for us here on earth.

Don't go there because if earth and or the actions of humans were clean, honest and righteous; we would see as well as abide with Lovey more than forever more.

Our sins have an impact on him hence keeping us from him.

It's one thirty three am June 06, 2015 and I so can't sleep. Slept already and dreamt I was cleaning but my bucket was broken. No not broken but I could not use the bucket properly. I am not one hundred percent sure, but I think in the same dream I peed myself. Weird because I was dreaming about Demons and or Satan the day before and my son was seeing them in reality. We were talking after he came home from school and he was asking me why he doesn't see happiness. Saying why he has to see demons. I don't know people because things we see in the living some of you cannot see. His demon and or the demon he saw was trying to scare him. He described the demon to me but I cannot help him when it comes to them. He told me he does not fear these demons anymore. He said, he was tired and just told this demon to go f himself. He said, he knows he's going to be angry and come back hence he won't go to sleep.

Wow because demons can be plagues in your life. This I know. I've told you in other books that I see faces. Sometimes when I close my eyes I see faces of people before me. Some are grotesque hence you see people before they die. I gather the grotesque faces are that of people who die bad.

Man if I could draw I would have a portfolio of the faces that I see, but I can't draw so you are spared the agony I see.

How do you stay sane you ask?

I don't let these faces bother me anymore. I don't even let the dead people I see in my dreams and or visions bother me anymore.

Demons don't bother me but they bother him because he's one child that do not listen to good counsel. Demons a nuh penny apinney I know this, but many in humanity do not know this. Hence I've told you, demons live to inflict pain. Pain is their natural high and sex.

Hopefully one day when he comes into his own with his spirituality these demons will leave him alone and not bother him so much.

So now you know demons are real and yes they have eyes of fire and or yellowish eyes.

But, but. There are no bobuts. Demons are real and they do exist. Hence you have to know the difference between Satan and demons.

Yes Satan has power but it is not Satan that posses, demons are the ones to do this. Demonic spirits are not the same as your human spirit. And I don't want to confuse you so I will stop right here because I will not be able to explain demonic possession properly for you to over stand and or understand and or comprehend.

I don't know if this is appropriate but I am going to say it anyway. Once you comprehend the spiritual you will comprehend the physical because both worlds interact with each other. Yes we have a spirit that connects to the spiritual world not just in sleep but in the waking hours as well.

We all have sight but for many their sight is clearer than yours. My sight is not the same as the person next door, hence we all have different visions; dreams in the waking hours and sleeping hours.

Hence wow because this book is wow to me. The higher hosts of hell are after me. This should not be a surprise to me because I've said some things in book nine that many globally will take offense to but I will not change my stance for anyone.

LISTEN, CERTAIN PEOPLE IN CERTAIN LANDS *I* WILL NOT SAVE BUT IT DOES NOT MEAN THAT LOVEY WILL NOT SAVE THEM.

Because I will not save these people does not mean that Lovey will not send someone else to save them.

My decision to not save someone if I am the saving grace of humanity is no reflection on Lovey. I am not going to be hypocritical in what I do for him. The burning of the Jamaica Flag did hurt me to the core. It hurt so bad that I told Lovey we were through, I am done with him and he told me yet again to write another book. So yes I did lodge my complaint with him. I took my displeasure to him in writing. So he has my record of truth before him.

MY CHOICE IS MY CHOICE AND NOT YOURS.
My displeasure is not your displeasure it's mine.
You have to live your life good and true but please,
DO NOT LET MY DISPLEASURE AFFECT YOUR
DECISION IN ANYTHING THAT YOU DO, DO
YOU HEAR ME.

Listen, the way things affect me is not the same way it affects you.

As humans we do not think.

Like I've told you in some of my other books, my greatest fear is losing Lovey. I do not want to displease him but I cannot live on pins and needles.

NEVER BE WORRIED ABOUT WHAT I SAY. THIS IS WHY I TELL YOU, IF YOUR RELIGION SUITS YOU, DO NOT LET ME HINDER YOU OR STOP YOU FROM GOING TO CHURCH. This is your truth and true love.

I'VE TOLD YOU, *ALWAYS BE TRUTHFUL TO LOVEY.* So if you go to the whore houses of death, and Lovey is the one you praise and give thanks to, then take your shoes off. *RESPECT IS DUE. LOVEY, GOOD GOD AND ALLELUJAH DESERVES OUR RESPECT AT ALL TIMES.*

I cannot sit with the wicked hence I tell you Psalms One is the psalms we are to live by. You cannot say you love and or truly love Lovey and commune with the wicked. You cannot live by double standards; you have to live by the standard and standards of Lovey, Good God and Allelujah.

Commune with good and clean people and discuss Lovey if this is your wish. *Hard will this be because no one can discuss Lovey in his truest and purest of form.* Lovey needs no discussion because he resides in us. Therefore we must live life good and true.

Like I said, people tell us to fear Lovey but why should we fear Lovey; the one we truly love? He's not a monster nor is he our abuser. Truly love him and you will see the beauty in your life.

Many of us love our husband and wife and we do not fear them, so why fear Lovey?

Yes I know the abuser in our lives but listen prayer, sincere prayer work. Never stop talking to Lovey, he will move you perfectly out of your abusive situation.

Listen, goodness does not come easily. Goodness comes at a price; cost to you. This is not because of Lovey, but because of wicked and evil people and spirits. Remember Lovey is trying to secure you and the devil and his people is doing all for you to fail in all that you do. One victory for Lovey is a blow to evil, hence evil will stop at nothing to make you fall and I've shown you this. Don't think Lovey has it easy because he does not have it easy with us humans. Look at the goodness he's given us and we've destroyed this goodness.

Lies are widely accepted globally hence there is so much sin on earth.

We can change this but for billions the damage is done and there is nothing anyone can do to save these people. Like I've said, I don't know why anyone would want to live to go to hell.

Why give your life over to Satan when you know once you've given him your life, your children and family belongs to him?

Why have kids if you are going to hand them over to death?

No one can get out of death's contract and we all know this. No, the ordained can free you but death will not forgive the ordained. This I know now. Like I said, we believe in lies and readily accept them without thinking of the consequences.

We believe liars that tell us, Lovey sacrificed his son to save wicked and evil people. And I keep asking; **_WHY WOULD LOVEY SACRIFICE HIS OWN TO SAVE WICKED AND EVIL PEOPLE?_**

Why should good people die to save wicked and evil people? This makes no sense to me.

Hell is there for everyone who is wicked and evil, so would Lovey sacrifice his own to death? I know for a fact that Lovey will never ever sacrifice his own for the Devil's own come on now.

Lovey has tried and is trying to save his own, so why would he hand his own over to the devil for a sacrifice?

What does death have to do with life?
Are they not two different things?

Is spiritual life not different from physical life?

Yes the life you live in the physical determines where you go in the spiritual, hence it's best to live in goodness and in truth. And don't go there, Lovey do not prevent you from having fun once the fun is clean. He will however prevent you from doing dirty things. For example, you love to go out dancing with your girlfriends. Lovey does not stop you from doing this. What he will stop you from doing is picking up someone in the club if you have someone at home and or if the person you are picking up is dirty if you do not have anyone and or someone at home. Respect goes a far and long way. If you are in a relationship with someone; respect your relationship and the person you are with.

We all have flaws and like you I am learning these things because some things mommy and daddy do not and or did not tell us. Some things we learn on our own. Mistakes happen, so truly learn from the mistakes you've made and teach your children not to make them if you have any kids and or children.

Listen people, the environment we live in is changing because time can never change. Time is constant. No one can lose time because time cannot lose. Our space is shrinking due to development and or population growth, the sinking of lands and or soil erosion, but time never; can never change. People change; grow hence the difference in time when it comes to humans. Human know not time hence we do not know the different time zones when it comes to the physical and spiritual world. We know not the spiritual hence we know not true time, cannot truly tell time in both worlds; the physical and spiritual world.

So yes I will piss off billions, but I truly do not care. You do not take away from life come on now. We as humans take from life and give to death and when things don't work out we cry to Lovey for a saving grace. Why take life from him if you are going to cry for help?

Why not do right and live?

In all the happenings that is happening on earth, was it truly worth it?

Is the fighting and hatred truly worth it?

We know about life and death but choose death anyway?

We say we don't want to die but yet live to die. What sense does that make? Life is worth living, we are the ones to give it away falsely.

We are the ones to say, here death take me. And don't you dare say no you didn't because you did. Look at your sins and or the wrongs you do on a daily basis and add them up.

No one should tell us to turn from life but yet we listen to people tell us to accept death and turn from life. Life gave you good and true life, so why turn from it, good and true life?

If you want better for self, do better for self. Walk in the truth and integrity of You and Good God come on now.

Love has no merit but truth, true love is valued most and or above all. This is because true love is rare and not everyone has truth. We say we have the truth but when it comes down to it, we have not truth but lies. (Your so called Holy Bible).

If your book was so true, why does it tell lies?
If your book was so holy, why do we sin?

If your book was so holy, why is it not saving humanity from all that is wicked and sinful; evil?

If your book was so holy, why do humans globally go against it?

If your book was so holy, why isn't humans living by life and not by death?

If your book was so holy and true, why isn't Lovey living amongst us and or living amongst humans globally?

And don't come to me with we are not all perfect, we are born in sin and shaped in iniquity.

NO, WE AS HUMANS CHOSE SIN FOR OUR CHILDREN AND WE ARE THE ONES TO SHAPE THEM IN INIQUITY.

And no, I will not take this statement back because it is true. Not one of us before we had our children went to Lovey in goodness and in truth and ask him for good clean, honest and true, truly loving and smart children. Children that is obedient. Children that would not walk in the way and ways of the sinful or wicked.

Children that would not stray from him or ever leave him.

Children that will go to him and cling to him in all that they do.

I didn't do this, you did do this; hence the devil and or Satan has billions of your children in the palm of his hands. So don't come tell me gibberish. You made the choice to sin and you have to accept this. No one can sugar coat it. You made a decision and it's this decision that you have to live by. Yes you can change this, but not all can change this. Many did sign a pact with the devil and or death and this pact and or contract is binding. No messenger can go to death and say, you have a signed contract for so and so and I want it.

No one can tell Satan or Death to tear up this contract. Not even Good God and Allelujah can do this. Hence I tell you what belongs to the devil and or death belongs to the devil and or death. Lovey cannot interfere nor will he interfere because you made a conscious decision to let Life; Him Lovey go.

No, no, no. He does. Just look at the youths of today. Some of them truly do not care hence they do all manner of evil to their parents and their fellow man.

I talk to my children and some don't listen hence the problems and trouble they get it.

My children are no different from yours hence I tell you about them. I'm not going to lie to you when it comes to them. Nor am I going to paint a pretty picture for you. Mi pickney dem damn bad. Meaning they do give trouble. No not all but some. Yes kids will be kids, hence the added stress they give you and me.

You have to take the good with the bad I know.
But do we truly have to? Man sometimes I wish there was a return button to send them back up the birth canal and never let them out. But unfortunately, things don't happen like in the movies. Fiction

So you do your best to raise your children and or child properly. I know it does not mean your children or child will follow good counsel because there are negative forces out there.

It's after three in the am and I have to try and get some sleep. Hungry but it's too early to make something to eat, and no I will not make a coffee.

Body isn't tired but need my rest.

Michelle

Yes it's a quiet day for me and stress is in the way but I won't let it get the best of me.

Tried talking to Lovey with the situation I am now in and failed. It's weird family, my life was just beginning to rise. Meaning my first two agreed to help me financially and now this.

Wow because I was blindsided. My child did not heed the warning signs and boom.

I truly do not understand why the now generation cannot listen. As a parent you see the dangers and warn them of the dangers, but yet they don't listen. Yes I am a worry wart and I don't think this will change but kids, you have to begin to listen to good counsel because things are not going to get better globally. Do not follow bad company come on now man. Certain things you are not ready for in life as a child or teenager, so don't put yourself into these unwanted situations. If you are in a good home stay in that good home and help your parents. Even if it's to do your chores and start dinner. Do it and help them (your parent or parents) to ease their burdens and or heavy load.

Some of you are in a one parent household. You see the hardships of your mom, help her to ease her burden, and do not add to it. The little you can do to help her goes a long way. I complain about my children and tell you of my frustrations with them. You don't have to be this way. You can help.

Do not X mama out of your life before time because when mama is gone, you are going to feel it hard if you are a disobedient child. Remember there is a tomorrow and tomorrow is guaranteed for everyone including wicked and evil people and spirits.

I know some of you are saying no it's not. But listen to me, tomorrow is guaranteed for everyone. It matters not if you die in the flesh today, your spirit still lives tomorrow. Life isn't just flesh it's spirit hence you were told to live in spirit and in truth. *THE PUNISHMENT YOU FEEL IN THE SPIRIT IS NOT THE SAME AS THE PUNISHMENT YOU FEEL IN THE FLESH.*

SPIRITUAL PUNISHMENT IS FAR MORE SEVERE AND THIS IS WHAT HUMANITY FORGETS. WE FORGET ABOUT THE SPIRITUAL WHICH IS VERY SAD.

LIFE DOES NOT END FOR GOOD AND TRUE PEOPLE, IT ONLY ENDS FOR WICKED AND EVIL PEOPLE AND SPIRIT.

And yes this is why some people tell you tomorrow is not promised, but know that tomorrow is guaranteed for the righteous; true and good people and spirits.

Yes this book was to be short and sweet but I've over extended my shortness by a lot of pages.

Oh yeah, I did say I was going to include what I did not put in book nine in this book; so here we go.

Listen, live your life good and true always and worry not about evil because prayer works. I've told you, Lovey is not a good teacher but he's an excellent protector. He does protect.

Financially, he's a lousy provider but this is from my stance. With him, certain things take time for me and I am the impatient one. Trust me when he blesses me financially, his land (s) and people will not be wanting of anything if I can help it. Like I've told you, my goodness goes towards his (our) people and lands including the universe. I do not do this for me alone. I have to hold your hands. Yes each and every one of you and take you to his world and or home. I will not leave you out if you belong to us. _**I truly more than infinitely and indefinitely do not need your soul and or spirit. Keep your soul and spirit but live good and true for you and your surroundings including children and family; Good God and Allelujah himself.**_ A place is prepared for me already by him, but I cannot reside alone with him. I need you with me in goodness and truth. *Like I've said, certain people in certain lands I will not save but it does not mean He Good God and Allelujah will not send someone to save the good and true people of these lands.* Goodness says a lot in Lovey's world, _**SO FRET NOT IF YOU ARE GOOD AND TRUE BECAUSE YOU DO BELONG.**_

Know that I will never ever take away the right and rights of a good and true; honest and clean people no matter the race colour or creed. This would be wrong on my part no matter how angry I get, and no matter what I write. Lovey, Good God and Allelujah is not that heartless and cold to do this. I am not that cold and heartless to do this.

There are laws that govern us and it's us as humans that refuse to live by these laws. And it's when we get punished we revert back to Lovey, Good God and Allelujah and expect him to fix our sins and or the lies we tell. We know the truth, because the truth is written but we refuse to follow these written truths. We refuse to do better for self.

Listen, no church or clergy can get you into the kingdom of Good God and Allelujah. You are the only one that can do this, so do the right thing for you and your family including friends come on now.

Lovey do not require churches of men, he requires your truth come on now.

I know some of you are saying; I do not believe in God because he does not hear me nor does he listen to me.

Some of you are saying; prayer does not work like my son. He got himself into his situation. He did not take telling; good counsel, so now he's stressing big time and he's a teen.

This is why I tell you it pays to listen to good counsel. Listen, I've made many mistakes in my life and I too did not listen to some of the good counsel my mother was instilling in me. I comprehend now; hence I try my best to do the good I can when I can.

I've also learned to listen to Lovey and I am trying to listen to the voice that screams at me when I am about to do something that is wrong. At times you will hear, "what you are doing is wrong." Yes Lovey does talk, so learn to listen to him because He will never steer you wrong. You can trust him in everything that you do. I am also trying to instill these good values into my children but it's hard. Ole people sey, when di harse gaane thru di gate eee haade fi ketch him. An ole people right. If you do not instill good values into your children when they are young, truly good luck in trying to instill these good values into your children when they get older. Think mindset and outside influences; friends people.

Prayer works, you are the one that is not listening to good counsel. You cannot go to Lovey and ask him for help and not come out of the situation you are in. He will tell you and show you what to do; you have to trust him and listen to him and not go back into the same situation.

You cannot say you want to leave your mistress and not take the right steps to leave her.

You cannot say that Lovey does not listen, because the good counsel your parent and or parents is giving you, you are the one not to listen. So when you do not listen to the good counsel of your parents then you are not listening to Lovey; Good God and Allelujah. ***A parent or parents that truly love cannot tell you to go out there and steal; do wrong.***

They cannot tell you to go out there and kill.

They cannot tell you to be ill mannered and or disrespectful to others despite how evil and wicked; cruel that person is.

TRUTH, GOOD AND TRUE LOVE DOES NOT PUT YOU IN BAD SITUATIONS NOR DOES TRUTH LIE; TELL LIES.

Like I said, we are the ones that do not listen to good counsel and when we get beat upon we run to Lovey, Good God and Allelujah for help.

We tell him to fix our situation and sometimes he cannot fix the situation for us.

Sometimes He let us fall on our own sword. See, Lovey has been trying and we are the ones to let things get out of hand.

What's done is done he cannot fix it. We are the ones that did not listen in the first place. It is only when we begin to amend our ways and walk on the pathway of goodness, truth and righteousness that we will see a positive difference in our lives.

What's broken is broken and no matter how you glue and or crazy glue that broken vase or vessel, that vase or vessel (you) is still broken. You cannot run around your problem or problems, you have to stand your ground and fix them.

You cannot run from them either. You have to slowly solve them until the problem is solved and or fixed. What you can do today, always do it and never put it off for tomorrow. Tomorrow is another day and different issues do arise.

It's like you hiring someone and say there's the computer do the work. If you do not show and or teach the person how to use the computer how is he or she going to know?

Not all computer languages are the same, hence different companies have different programs to suit their need and needs. Life is like this in many ways.

Lovey is there for everyone but it's not everyone that is there for Lovey and we all know this.

Different cultures have different customs and gods. Hence my god may not be right for you. So in life, do what makes you truly happy but insure that in all of your doing, you are clean, good and honest. You have to be truthful in all that you do. Yes you may lose family and friends, but in truth, *TRUTH CANNOT LOSE TRUTH.* If a person is not truthful you will lose them, but if they are truthful and honest; good; you cannot lose them.

I've told you I've made Lovey my bestest of friend and it's going to stay this way forever ever despite what I write sometimes. You cannot lose truth if you are truthful come on now.

ALL THAT LOVEY REQUIRES FROM US IS OUR TRUTH AND HONESTY NOTHING ELSE.

What about love you are saying?

Lovey does not require love, he requires true love.

There are no but buts about this. I truly love you.

Would I go out of my way to hurt you?

No.

If I did, I would not have truly loved you. True love is precious to me because it's so rare that when you have it, you do not want to let it go or lose it.

You do not go out of your way to hurt the next person and or individual.

Yes you will have fears when it comes to Lovey and that fear is losing him. You do not want to lose him hence you think of him and the consequences associated with your wrong and or bad actions. It's not to say in the heat of the moment and or in an angry state you don't say hurtful things. I do when I am angry. These books, well some of them are a testament of my anger and pain. But when all is said and done, I go to Lovey. I take my anger and frustrations out on him.

He can't blame me for this. Like I said, I would rather go to him than go to man with my issues, and I do go to him with all. Yes I speak to family but Lovey is my first and foremost go to.

I more than need him hence he's important in my life. I cannot let him go despite me telling him I am going to. I just can't. There's something about Him that I need. He's vital to and in my life. Yes it's hard and it's hard to listen to good counsel but try.

Take things day by day by taking baby steps to Him Lovey and Good God. He's your Allelujah come on now. He cannot be anything but our ***BREATH OF LIFE.*** So make Him your life choice because Death is ready and waiting, and trust me, death do take by any means necessary. Malcolm X

Ah Lovey, what can I say to you apart from truly help me and guide me on the path of righteousness in my time of need. My son need you right now and I need you too. You are the best healer I know hence I am asking you to show us what to do. I am in a state of confusion because something is not right somewhere, but yet I don't know what to do. Please guide my me and my son on the right path.

We are both stressing and you know my tears and fears. Hence I ask why Lovey, why do these kids do not listen to good and true counsel. None of us can go back into the past and undo our wrongs.

None of us can right the wrongs and or mistakes of our past, but yet I cannot comprehend why a child would not take good counsel in this day and time. Yes I know my past and my past wrongs and disobedience, but I've tried with mine just as how you are and have tried with humanity.

Lovey, tell me and my son what to do so that we can move forward in a positive and true way.

Lovey we are both lost in this. Maybe it's me that can't come to grips with this because I am not ready. Hence stressed am I.

Stressed is my son. So please guide us and help us come to grips with this; our situation. Let this be a learning process for the both of us as well.

Lovey many things humans are not ready for. Right now billions are not ready for you, so what's going to happen when death comes on a massive scale?

If they are not ready for you now, how are they going to be ready for you when death come Lovey?

Humans are not prepared for this destruction. It's coming, and yes we are to blame. Hence many are going to be left behind.

Lovey, we did this to self due to our sins. The churches of the globe won. They gave death the victory over humanity because they did lie as well as sacrificed their own to death for a place in hell.

Lovey, listen to the song WORLD PEACE by Nature. Tell me something, if a nation of people has no peace in them, how can they say they are peaceful?

How can they cry out Allah when they take life from the Breath of Life; You?

When did Allah and or Allelujah become death?

ABSOLUTELY NO ONE CAN KILL FOR LIFE LOVEY YOU AND I KNOW THIS. PEOPLE CAN ONLY KILL FOR DEATH, A PLACE IN HELL AND BILLIONS HAVE THEIR PLACE IN HELL WAITING FOR THEM LITERALLY.

I was told to come home by this white man. *YES I KNOW THAT WHEN I SEE WHITE PEOPLE IN MY DREAM STATE, THAT WHITE PERSON CAN BE BLACK IN THE LIVING.*

Yes it's hard to explain for humanity to comprehend hence I tell them, some whites are blacks and some blacks are white. Yes it's confusing to them but if they know not spirituality then they will be more than confused. Confused am I but for my son. It's a confusing state to be in hence I leave everything in your capable hands.

As humans billions know right from wrong but yet billions choose to do wrong anyway.

I cannot comprehend humanity on a whole. Why kill for a place in hell?

What is so great about hell that you have to die to go there?

Look at the different nations on a whole Lovey and tell me what is wrong with man; humanity that we cannot learn and live good with one another?

<u>The fighting is not necessary Lovey because no one can fight and or kill to get to you. When we fight and kill we are locking self, land and the other people of our land out of your kingdom and abode.</u>

Lovey why don't we know this?
What's so hard about learning this?

Hence I leave all in your good and capable hands. Only you can fix this Lovey, but how is the question?

Michelle

Oh man the back pains are getting so severe when I walk. It never used to be like this, now the pain is here.

Lower back pain sucks.
Yes I lay on my back but still the back pain sucks.
It's as if the pain is moving up my spinal column.

Man I can't take it anymore.

Wow my tummy feels as if it's getting bigger and yes I am gaining weight and I hardly eat that much. Have cut back a lot but still I am gaining weight and I can feel it in my hips.

When I walk it's as if my hip is pressing against my lower spinal column.

Yes the pain is real and I so need to get rid of it naturally,

Michelle
May 27, 2015

Ah man I am so done for.

Lovey why does sickness have to come?

Why do I have to feel so much back pain?

I know this is not your doing, but couldn't you do something for me like find me a real good masseuse that will work all my kinks, aches and pain out?

Ah Lovey the joy of being one sucks sometimes.

Can I run away from you and all? I mean, can I go to some world that is safe from harm, sickness and all facet of pain?

Lovey pain sucks; hence I truly hate my lower back pain.

Michelle
May 27, 2015

Lovey, why is sex so strong?

Why do we think dirty things; thoughts?
Why are our thoughts not clean; pure?

Lovey, why is sex so powerful that it causes men to leave their wives; girlfriend and women to leave their husbands; boyfriend?

Should sex not be pure; clean?
So why is it not pure and clean?

Was sex meant to be this way?

I know I am not having any but isn't masturbation a form of sex and pleasure?

Yes masturbation is a sin due to thoughts but isn't truth apart of our culture?

Do we (some of us) not ask you for a good and clean partner and you neglect us? So if we are true to this form of pleasure, why sin us for it?

Do you not leave us to find pleasure elsewhere?

Lovey pure thoughts, but with sex the thoughts are not pure why?

Why Lovey, why?

You are the Breath of Life but yet you do not teach us about sex and clean thoughts. So how are we to live when we do not truly know what's clean and wholesome; pure to you?

So in all I've taught, why neglect sex, masturbation and foreplay?

I've talked about homosexuality, but what is clean sex to you?

What is clean masturbation to you?

What is clean foreplay to you?

Michelle
May 27, 2015

No Lovey I do not want to hide my thoughts from you and I refuse to.

I refuse to sweep anything under the rug because we are truly not this way.

I come to you with everything, so teach me everything good and true; clean and positive.

I need to know what is clean sex and clean love making to you.

Lovey, sex is a powerful tool that the body and spirit needs. So why shy away from this topic? I need to know the truth.

Do you fear us leaving you for him her?

Do you fear us becoming unclean and losing our place with you?

Lovey, if we do not know the truth, will we not do all that is wrong?

Are we not doing all that is wrong right now?

Do we not come to different crossroads daily and choose badly?

So how can you sin us if we know not the truth?

False teachings are there, but if we do not know the truth, will we not follow these false teachings?

So Lovey, teach me the truth about sex, true sex and making love; love making.

I do not want or need dirty teachings Lovey, I need clean teachings.

Lovey like I've told you, my greatest fear is losing you. So I need to know about sex, clean sex and staying true to you.

I cannot run from this topic nor can I hide from it anymore.

You are my keep so truly do right by me and teach me about clean sex and making love and or love making indefinitely.

Michelle
May 27, 2015

Ah Lovey I truly don't know but what is spiritual and physical pleasure combined?

Can we attain both at the same time?

Can the physical and spiritual be on the same level at the same time here on earth given the amount of sins being done by us humans on a daily basis?

Lovey, what is the point of life if death and sorrow is all around?

What is the point of life if we cannot have physical life and spiritual life on the same accord for all who are good and true?

Lovey, what is the point of having you if we cannot have you here on earth with us?

I know you need your mega mansion, but in giving you this mega mansion, will you let evil come and destroy it?

Are you going to permit wicked and evil people and spirits to come in and take it from you; us?

If so, what is the pint of giving you a mega mansion if evil is going to have a way in?

Lovey I truly don't know. I want and need to be totally clean and pure for you but I have blemishes on my sin plate; record.

Lovey, why couldn't you have made me pure and void of all sins?

Ah Lovey, cherish me like I cherish you.

Yearn and desire me like I yearn and desire you.

You are my place
My trees and waters
You are my all.

Michelle and Michelle Jean
May 27, 2015

I am but a tree
You see me but you cannot hear me

We speak the same language but you do not know
how to communicate with me

I sway this way and that way
I laugh
I cry, but to you I am but a simple tree without feel;
a voice.

Michelle (Mom)
May 27, 2015

I am but a tree
Can you hear my voice?

Yes you can feel me
Feel the breeze beneath me
But can you hear me?
Hear my voice?

Do you even know how to communicate with me?

Have you ever tried speaking to me?
Laughing with me?

I like music just like you
I truly like peace and quiet
How about you?

I like water; it cools me down and helps me to grow.
What about you, does water do the same thing for
you?

It does. Then we are so much alike. But with you,
you hurt and destroy me without knowing me. So
why do you hate me without knowing me?

What have I done to you for you to hurt me so?

From a tree to you by Michelle Jean
May 27, 2015

Ah Lovey I wish you could have breakfast with me each and every morning, lunch and dinner too including snacks.

Yes you would feel how I feel health wise, but this is not the reason for me saying this.

You are my world
Need and wants

Well I can't make you all that I wear including underwear, but if I could I would.

Smile because the crazy and insane me is back but only briefly. Need more logic; my quiet time with you.

Ah Lovey what a day? Well the day is just beginning. Yes the tummy is burning slightly and it's beginning to feel sore, but that's me on some given and or certain given days.

It pays to be healthy and not sick.

Lovey, why does my body have to be so sick? There are days when I cannot go.

Have no energy to go.
Cannot walk.

There are days when my feet cannot carry me literally.

I worry not about my future mobility. It's the sugar that is uncontrollable that I worry about.

Ah Lovey, I need some true time with you.

I need more access to you.
I truly hope you are not like the men of today.

Physical and spiritual men that are whores.

Well I know you're not but I had to bring that in the mix. You know me and my thinking sometimes.

Cray, Cray yeah that's me. Well at times with you anyway.

Michelle
May 28, 2015

Ah Lovey, what a day; well not a day because the morning is in full swing.

Lovey, am I different from you?
I mean do you think the way I do sometimes?

I know you are far more intelligent than me. Yes superior in thought, planning, action, implementation, getting things done, but do you think like me at times?

Do you want and need true peace and harmony?

If so, what's stopping you from achieving this for me, you and our good and true people?

Why let evil progress?
Why let evil move forward and destroy?

I know we as humans make bad choices, but why let us continue to defame and disgrace you; make bad choices?

I know Will and negative energy have the greater pull, but why can't you eliminate our negative will and thoughts here on earth if we've asked you to?

Lovey, I know we do not all belong to you, but can't you truly shut down all facets of evil right now?

Why should your good and true people share the same space with them (wicked and evil people and spirits) or even breathe the same air?

Evil pollutes.

Who needs wicked and evil people including wicked and evil societies?

Michelle and Michelle Jean
May 28, 2015

One day of happiness; the next day is war with me and my children, hence I am holding my peace Lovey.

I had a good week with my daughter, now all hell is ready to erupt because it seems her demons have come back and war is about to break out between me and her. Hence I can't wait until I have a place for myself and they have to fend for their own; pay their own bills just like me.

Lovey, my last two WOW and that's all I got to say.

You did warn me about the father but I could not comprehend your warning; hence good and evil did meet and procreate and I paid the price literally.

I don't have to talk. Those that know me can tell you of the evils and hell I've faced; hence Behind the Scars is just a tat of what I've faced – the hell I've been through and still going through.

I can't face anymore hence I am holding on to LIFE by a thread literally. Many mornings I can't go but I keep going – try; thus I keep telling my children one day they are not going to have me because I am sicker than they think. But with everything else they don't listen to me. Hence they are not prepared and will never be prepared for the day when I leave them indefinitely.

Yes I know my end with them and it's unfortunate that my last two cannot see this. They don't hear nor do they listen.

My second one is coming into his own hence he talks to you a lot now Lovey. He's beginning to know and see things. You are directing him and I truly thank you for this and him. It has been a rough and bumpy ride for the both of us but we are making it slowly.

You are his guide so continue to guide him right and truthful.

My first guide and protect him also. Guide and protect him right. Teach them right.

Be their good and true blessings because they need you as much as I do.

As for my last two, I put them in your good and true hands as I do my first two.

Michelle
May 30, 2015

It's been a up and down ride with you Lovey but I am still holding on. I have to hold on because our journey is far from over.

The dreams are coming and I have to pray and ask you for mercy. I have to pray and ask you for guidance and protection of those that are in our kingdom of truth.

I have to pray and ask you for guidance and protection of all those who will now join our kingdom of truth. Lovey, protect Fred Hammond for me because you know how I feel about this man's music and how his music soothe me on any given day.

Dreamt we knew each other, meaning was beginning to talk as friends. He had a concert. I saw him singing on stage and I wanted to go and talk to him but I refrained. I did not want the now President of the United States to kill him because he knew Fred Hammond knew me.

So in all I'm asking Lovey. I ask you to protect each and every one (good and true people) that will now come around me. I ask you to protect those that will now try to get to know you in goodness and in truth. You know the devil will not stand and or will not lose any (a soul) to you. ***You and I know that***
NO CHURCH ON THE FACE OF THIS

PLANET AND IN THE UNIVERSE UNITE PEOPLE. ALL CHURCHES AND OR THE CLERGY DO IS DIVIDE AND CONQUER IN THE NAME OF SIN; THE DEVIL; HELL.

Lovey you and I know the agenda of wicked and evil people, hence wicked and evil people know not you nor do they know your goodness and truth.

Evil divide and conquer hence many races; black race have been divided and conquered; given filth and languages of filth that are not their own.

Many have lost their land and history; heritage and place with you because of religion. And instead of saying no, this is not what Lovey, Good God and Allelujah wants, billions continue to trust and follow religion blindly to hell.

Many would rather live in ignorance rather than know the truth. I know the truth. I know the truth of wicked and evil lands and people. I also know if evil cannot get into your kingdom and abode, evil was going to do all to keep them (my people as well as good and true people) from you but humanity cannot see this. *HUMANITY IS BANKING ON YOUR SON TO SAVE THEM.*

HUMANITY BOUGHT INTO TO JESUS LIE AND NOW LOOK AT THE EARTH TODAY.

- *NO ONE SEES THE TRUTH*
- *NO ONE KNOWS THE TRUTH*
- *NO ONE WANT TO KNOW THE TRUTH*
- *IGNORANCE SUITS HUMANITY JUST FINE, HENCE THEY BREAK YOU UP AND DIVIDE YOU UP INTO THIS RELIGION AND THAT RELIGION. NO ONE CAN SEE THAT YOU ARE NOT A RELIGION. THEY ARE NOT A RELIGION BUT LIFE; GOOD AND TRUE LIFE.*
- *THEY CANNOT SEE THAT YOU LOVEY IS GOOD AND TRUE LIFE THAT WANTS WHAT'S BEST FOR ALL.*

All these things humans cannot see and this is truly sad. Hence please truly protect those that will now join you indefinitely. Protect them from all that is wicked and evil including wicked and evil spirits and people. Lovey, be their defence force because I will not have evil hurting anyone because of me or you. Evil have to stay their course hence none (no evil) must come in our direction or the direction of our good and true people. All that evil do and does to hurt us Lovey, let it infinitely and indefinitely forever ever without end turn back on them; evil. The time of evil is over and your good and true people must now live in goodness and in truth forever ever without end infinitely and indefinitely. I did not come into your fold of goodness and truth for you to allow evil, wicked and evil spirits and people to continue to hurt goodness and truth, good and true people and spirits. I've told you, true love does not hurt nor can it cause pain. If you as God, Good God and Allelujah do not mean us any good, then truly stay the hell away from us because you are not true; nor are you real. You are a fake and fraud because true goodness is not in you and never was in you from the get go. You are my goodness and truth hence I ask you to secure good and true places for me and your good and true people. Evil I leave alone to time; their own brutal end and you know this. So do right and just by me and your good and true people.

Death has secured a place in hell for their wicked and evil own and it's now time for you to secure a good and true place for your own in your kingdom and abode as well as your good and true land and lands more than infinitely and indefinitely forever ever without end. So because of this, death and all facets of evil must be gone from us as well as be gone from around us more than infinitely and indefinitely more than forever ever without end.

You can no longer permit evil to destroy and kill us come on now. What is the point of walking and talking with you, if you are going to allow evil people and spirits to continue to hurt and keep down your good and true own?

What are you telling me?

Are you telling me evil is greater than you?
Hath more power than you?

Are you telling me evil created this earth and universe?

Are you telling me, as God, Good God and Allelujah, you're evil's and or death's bitch that death can use at will?

No Lovey, I am angry at you and forgive me if I've stepped out of line because you know me when I am angry. I have to take my anger out on you because you are the only one I know. You are my all hence I need you and your true goodness and peace in my world which is our world.

In all I've asked of you Lovey, why can't you hear me and listen to me truthfully?

Why do you take so long in helping me?
Why do you take so long to answer me?

There are days when I feel powerless.

Days when I think you are powerless; hath no power when it comes to wickedness; sin and evil.

Yes I know this is wrong on my part but you leave me with no other option. Look at what I am seeing Lovey. I am back in the confusing state because all I see is confusion in my personal life and I now have to ask you why?

Why should my personal life be left in confusion and disarray?

Why are there lies between me and you in my personal life?

Why am I being lied to in my dream world?
Why am I being confused in my dream world?

What is the purpose of me having you in my life when you're confusing me; can't give me true stability; freedom and peace; true peace?

I don't need confusion around me. I need the good and true you without the confusion and disarray.

So in all that you do Lovey, think of our good and true people. Think of their good and true life.

Think of the good and true me.

You cannot let evil harm any of them including me and my immediate and or biological family. I am trying but you are allowing evil to wipe out and this cannot be. You are defeating the purpose; my efforts when it comes to you.

You cannot tell me about praise and cleanliness and leave us in unclean lands. You have to find a way to get our good and true people out of defiled and condemned lands; lands that are unclean come on now.

You told me Jamaica was unclean and you will not allow me to go into this land, so why are you allowing your good and true people; own to stay in wicked and unclean land and lands?

Should we not be cleaning up our good and true people and take them to the safe havens of your good and true land and lands; kingdom and abode?

Lovey I truly don't know with you anymore sometimes.

Also dreamt Lady Saw again. We were discussing cheating and she said, "A cheater will always cheat," and she is correct. People that cheat do not care about you. Nor do they care about their partner. Cheating has become the norm with man; humans that we care not for the relationships they are in. Self gratification is all many think about. Yes I am getting wiser and older as the days and years go by, but Lovey, why do we truly forget about you?

WHY DO WE CHEAT?
WHY DO WE CHEAT ON YOU?

Why do we show you and your laws so much disrespect?

I've sinned and I am no different from the next man or woman out there. But I am learning to truly know you and it's not an easy road. Like I said, evil eliminates good people. Evil want this earth and universe for self.

Evil do not care about the good of man. All evil cares about is the evils of man. The more evil and or wickedness the person do and or does, the longer that person's spirit stay in hell and burn. Hence prolonging the life of death and or evil in hell.

I also dreamt I was in this place and I went walking. There were vendors on the side walk and this white man, skinny and wearing police like clothing was directing young and older white people dressed in jouvert clothing, and or mass costumes, and or mardi grass and or carnival costumes. Wow you should see the people so happy and doing their thing. Hence if my niece asks me to follow her to Caribana this year I will not go. Walking on the side walk there were fruits, food of the Caribbean nature and I wanted to buy some. I also saw these beautiful chains and bracelets that Rasta's sold. Lovey they were beautiful but I never bought any. I wanted to buy some fruits and food but did not get any in my initial walk. I saw some guinep and went to buy some but the man that sold them was almost sold off. I could not get any of what he had left because he had a small amount. So he said he had to go into the fridge to get some more. The young girl that was working with him said, go into the fridge. We both thought it weird that he had to go into the fridge to get more guineps. Suffice it to say, I did not wait on him. I left and went into another area that had lots of Caribbean fruits and food. Going into this area this man saw me and gave me this big bag of guinep. The lady that was with him said, what did you do that for?

Yes I ate some and it tasted sour and or stale in my mouth. Apparently the lady he was with was his sister. He had liked me but could not approach me I guess. She the sister was telling me he's 48 and much older than me. I told her, he's not older than me, I am older than him. She said you're 50 and I said yes I am. She told me her brother's name but I cannot remember it. All I know was, he was tall and was in dark clothing. Including the little girl I mentioned was in dark clothing but she (this lady) was in white and black. More like a zebra coloured maxi dress. Trust me she had a nice shape because she was slender. I can't remember if she had really low cut hair but that's neither here nor there. In the dream I gave him (this guy) my number for which he wrote in an exercise book. He tore out a few pages out of the book and said he did not need these anymore. His sister and myself scolded him for doing that because he was going to throw away the pages on the ground. From his look and or persona he did not like us scolding him about throwing away those pages in his exercise book. She also said to me, their mother or grandmother would have liked me. In the dream I wondered if he was working and or what job he did.

After scolding him this younger white man came around and was telling the people to pack up because the venue was closing up. It was time for everyone to go. *And family I am sorry for the odd way I've written this dream. If I've confused you, it's not intentional. My writing is just weird and trust me I too confuse myself with my writings at times. So truly forgive me.*

Wow because something is so not right in my personal life. Sour grapes now spoiled guinep.

Lovey, I truly do not know what's going on in my life. I've told you something is truly not right and I don't know if this has to do with my son and what he's going through right now.

And Lovey, I dreamt a few days back my first two's grandmother. She was telling me I am not welcomed at her home; she never wanted to see me again. And in all honesty Lovey, I truly do not care if my family disowns me for these books.

I truly do not care if they don't want to have anything to do with me and my children. I walk alone and will always walk alone; hence I am alone with you in all that I do.

I also don't give a bleep if the black community or the white community rise up against me globally. I know the evils and anger of man; hence Satan and his band of trolls will come after me.

I am not here to win a popularity contest. If humanity rejects the truth yet again then so be it. You just weren't meant to be Lovey. Rejection we are both used to, so you have to leave humanity alone. I will not die for anyone. I would rather walk away from you in truth, true truth, peace, true peace, goodness and cleanliness than die for you or anyone. Life, good life is valued. You can die for humanity if you want to Lovey, but I will not die for any because I know the preciousness of life.

You are precious to me not humanity due to wickedness and sin. You know who truly love and care for you. Accept us, the ones that truly care and love you.

Do not waste your breath and save people that are not deserving of you. You know who these undeserving people are but yet you do not follow *YOUR LAW AND LAWS OF TRUTH WHEN IT COMES TO TRUE LOVE, GOOD AND TRUE LIFE; GOODNESS AND TRUTH.*

The truth does not hurt Lovey and I will never ever apologize for what's written in these books. If people want to hate me and try all to set me up and kill me that's their problem and not mine. I know hell is there. So when I am safe with you and drinking of your pure waters of life and eating your good fruits, they'll be in hell burning worse than a bitch in heat.

I cannot worry about wicked and evil people because I know and you know they have no place with you. So if family members disown me, it's their loss and my gain.

It's your gain as well because I've tried my best to stay true to you. I've done all to be truthful to you in all that I do. I cannot be like anyone, I have to be me. I have to be quirky and true to you.

Evil has tried with me but because of truth I've stayed with you.

You've always been there for me even when I cry and blast you; tell you you are unfair.

I've even told you I hated you in my anger.

I've always walked a lonely road with you Lovey and you've kept me, kept me sane in all of this.

There are days when I feel I can't make it.
Days when I feel as if I am going to go insane due to stress overload. But with all that is happening in my life, I tell you about it and here I am. *So* **whatever my family say and do it matters not to me as long as I have you and my children as well as the good and true seeds you have and has given to me.**

I am not here to hurt anyone and if people think this way then so be it. I cannot change the way they think nor can I change the way they feel.

I cannot save everyone because in truth, not all in life belongs to you. Billions of people including spirits made the choice to follow death and it's by death that they live.

You never gave any of us religions of men to condemn and kill self and family including others by. You gave us good and true life without blemishes. We as humans put blemishes on our slate and or in our lives. We cannot blame you for the happenings of this world because we were categorically told, "THE WAGES OF SIN IS DEATH."

We let others misguide us and I refuse to misguide anyone when it comes to true life and you. So if my family deny me, so be it. Yes I will cry at first but I will get over it. As long as I have you beside me in all that I do, then I am more than good to go.

Yes my anger gets the best of me at times but this is me when it comes to you. I am in a learning process and I would like all in humanity to choose you, but this is wishful thinking on my part. Like I said, not all in humanity belongs to you.

Some are of the dead due to choice as well as family choice, and I will not be this way. I will not walk on the pathway of death and pretend to like and or love you. I cannot do this nor will I do it. You do not lie to anyone. Humans tell lies on you not the other way around and I cannot be like these people. Yes I know I have to go through hardships. I go through it and bare it, so that our good and true people don't have to. This is why I tell you, we need to secure good and true land and lands for them. *Every nation has their own god Lovey; hence you are not the choice of billions.*

I do not need the WHITE MAN'S GOD.

I do not need the HINDU'S GOD.

I do not need the MUSLIM GOD.

I do not need the EUROPEAN GOD.

I NEED MY BLACK GOD, THE BLACK MAN'S GOD AND THAT GOD IS TRULY YOU ALLELUJAH.

You are the god that created it all as well as maintain it all and I have you. So why would I want another's god? God's that are dead and taken from our true *BLACK HISTORY; CULTURE AND HERITAGE.* And if any of you feel that I am racist to say this, that's fine. My god is not based on colour; hue, hence no racism is in the words I mentioned. If you want to take yourself out of this go right ahead. But you that are of the truth should know better, say and do better.

Why should anyone suffer because of wicked and evil people and spirits?

Now I ask you this. Why do you make it so hard for me in all that I do for you?

Do you not appreciate what I am trying to do for you?

Do you not cherish our good and true people?

If you do, why make life in the living so hard for them; us?

Why should I have to cry to you and suffer bouts of stress and doubt when it comes to you and my surroundings?

Yes you want to show us how hard it is when we do not have you. I get this, but in doing so, are you saying our hardships is your way of saying we don't truly have you?

No, this could not be hence I've asked an incorrect question. Yes I know many of us go through it so that your people and or our people don't have to. But there has to be more Lovey. There just has to be more. We need true unification of our people so that every good that we do grow positively as well as help our good and true community as a whole.

Lovey, why can't my goodness be added to her and his goodness so that over time, the universe and this world, earth is clean and void of all evil and evils; sin and despair; hardship?

Shut wickedness and evil down now man, come on Lovey. Grow in truth with me and your people which is our people. You know we need you, but yet you are separated from us due to the wickedness and sins of others and this is truly not fair.

Yes I know wicked and evil people and spirits wants us to fail and this is beyond me. *If you say you want life, WOULD YOU NOT DO ALL THAT IS GOOD AND TRUE IN YOUR POWER TO SECURE LIFE?*

Why abandon life?

If Lovey has and have sent someone to secure you, why not help that person to secure you and your future?

Why be ignorant?

Yes I've encountered ignorant people in life while on the pathway of truth, and these are the people I truly do not want or need to know. Truth means nothing to them, so why would I want to be around them or even secure them?

You do not fight for death, you live your life good and clean come on now.

Lovey never told anyone to fight and kill their brothers and sisters; the next person. We all did this on our own because of hate. I refuse to take up arms against anyone. You can more than kiss my natural brown ass if you think I am going to take up arms against you. You're not bleeping worth it nor are you worth the time and effort. Kiss it bitches because it's my world and word with Lovey and not yours. You don't belong because He's infinitely and indefinitely more than forever ever without end locked your ass out. I know hell is your infinite and indefinite home, so why would I take up arms against you?

You hurt me dearly and I want nothing to do with you, hence I will not save you. Do not look to me for a saving grace because when you hate me, you hate Lovey also. All I do in goodness and in truth is to secure him and our good and true people. It's for him and our people also, so why wouldn't I go to him with all?

I go to him with my evil thoughts too because I care. I do not want or need evil thoughts hence I write and tell you all these things.

Like I've said, I will not save wicked and evil people nor will I save certain people in certain lands,

but <u>*IT DOES NOT MEAN HE WILL NOT SEND SOMEONE ELSE TO SAVE YOU.*</u>

Yes I tell him not to send anyone else to save humanity, but this decision to send someone else is not up to me, it's up to him because it's his world and kingdom.

I will not take away the right and rights of good and clean people; those who are trying to be good. It's not fair on my part to do this.

Every individual have a saving grace in this world and it's up to us to use our saving grace and or life line wisely. Yes billions gave up this saving grace by accepting death in the living but I worry myself not about these people. ***WHAT'S DONE IS DONE AND I WILL NOT INTERFERE AND CHANGE THIS.*** You went against goodness and continued on your evil path. So because of this, you must pay and will pay dearly.

Good and true life isn't about cheating anyone.

Good and true life is not about whoredom; death, it's about good life. We had good life and billions gave this good life up for naught and this is truly a shame.

WE AS HUMANS ARE THE ONES THAT CANNOT BE SATISFIED WITH WHAT WE HAVE.

We want what the next man has. I don't, hence I do not live my life on the terms set out by men. I live my life for me and Lovey based on our truth and truths that are set out for all including Him.

I cannot live to hurt people and I refuse to. If you don't want me in your country, wey mi a guh eggsup fa an come inna fiyu country?

You truly don't like black people, then truly do not look for a black person to come and save you because we won't. I won't despite my lineage and or descent; heritage. I fall under the banner of Black that which is the banner of Lovey, Good God and Allelujah, so why would I go against him and disrespect him for you?

You are not worth it, hence I step aside from you and hold on to Lovey more than infinitely and indefinitely.

Every kingdom Lovey gives an opportunity to be saved. It's up to that nation and or kingdom to accept or reject his messengers. My homeland rejected their messengers.

America, the United States of America rejected their messengers.

Africa, Mama Africa, some of her lands rejected Lovey and side with Evil. Mama Africa asked me for prayer and she received it because she is tired of what's happening in Africa.

I told you, I will not save any Nigerian because of what those scumbags in Nigeria are doing to their

Nigerian Own. And this is if I am the saving grace for humanity. I know the hatred the Babylonians have for Black People and or the Black Race. So why would I save anyone who have joined forces with them to disgrace, kill and or massacre their own and disrespect Lovey and his laws?

You are not black you are death come on now.
We say we are blacks but readily turn our backs on Lovey and accept all that is Pagan and demonic.

We say we love but yet pick up arms to kill others including our own.

Everyone has forgotten, 'THE WAGES OF SIN IS DEATH."

When we kill each other we die. Death must come tomorrow to take you and it matters not if tomorrow is two years from now or 24 000 years. You must die.

Your spirit must leave the flesh for you to be sentenced in the grave. We made it this way because we were to walk to Lovey and or walk back to Lovey in flesh and spirit. We weren't supposed to lose the flesh. No shedding of blood and flesh is required from or by Lovey. But because of sin, we've defiled ourselves and become unclean. We walked away from cleanliness and now look at humanity today?

Look at what we've become due to the lies and deceit of others including other nations.

We were the ones to make the choice to lose him; so no one on the face of this planet can blame him for our failings.

No one can say Lovey did this and this to me that is evil. Lovey is not evil humans are.

We want to control others and this is wrong.

Why should you tell me how to live and or praise the one that I truly love and more than adore with my all and everything if I already know him and have him?

I am living a clean and pure life that is good and true, so why are you taking me from it and him? These are the things we as humans don't look into and do for self and Lovey, Good God and Allelujah.

If I am safe with him, why tell me to choose death? Would you not tell me to choose life and live life good and clean come on now?

You want good and better for self, why not want good and better for me also? Come on now.

Life isn't one sided, so why are you making life one sided?

Lovey isn't impartial, so why are you letting me think that he is?

Lovey wants what's right and best for you, so why not want and need what is right and best for him also?

He's trying, so why are you breaking him down?

We have hope, so why live like the hopeless?

Why live in fear?

Did Lovey tell anyone of us to fear him?

So why fear him?

You say you fear him but yet do all that is sinful and wrong. So how is that fear? Yes we all make mistakes but mistakes are tools we can all learn from and by. We know this this and this is a mistake; learn from it and don't make these mistakes again. Teach your children and others of these mistakes if you can so that they don't make them.

We say we are our brothers and sisters keeper, but in truth NONE, NOT ONE OF US KEEP OUR BROTHERS AND SISTERS. And don't you dare say otherwise, because we truly don't. We fight and argue amongst each other when we don't have to.

My brother and sister treats me unfair. Well stay away from them. My sister said something I did not like about my mother and I told her I would never come back to her house again. I've kept my word until this day. If I find you offensive and or if you hurt me, I cut you off indefinitely. Meaning things I did with you I will not do it. You are off limits. I am still there for my sister, but going to her house I will not go because my word is my word. If my sister wants help, I will help her but I will not go to her house. I told her I am never coming back there. Yes I am stubborn in many ways but I live by my word. Sometimes I fail at my word, but things that burn me to the core I will not back down from. My mother I more than universally truly love hence I harp about her. You and Lovey know this hence I do my all to save her. Some of my goodness have to go to her because she was more than there for me when I needed her.

When the devil came with his smoke and fire to kill me, she was the one that was right there holding my hand. She warned him, but he did not heed his warning and now he's in hell burning like a bitch.

This is why I cannot give up on Lovey and my more than gorgeous mother. I more than unconditionally and universally truly, truly more than truly love them with all my truth. They are more than my world and I cannot give them up for anyone or anything. I have to do all to make them happy as well as save them. Truth isn't about hate, it's about truth.

TRUTH IS EVERLASTING LIFE AND WE ALL KNOW THIS. BUT INSTEAD OF LIVING BY THE TRUTH, WE LIVE BY SINS; LIES AND EXPECT LOVEY TO SAVE US.

It's like my second son said to me today, (June 08, 2015), God helps us mom, we are the ones to make him cry. We are the ones that don't think of him.

When we don't listen he's not there to help us because he tried and we did not listen. And he's so correct. We make mistakes and we are to learn from them.

The choice we make in our lives we are the ones to make them and we can't blame God or anyone else for these choices. He also said we can't blame us, but we have to blame us because we are the ones to make the wrong choice.

We talked about other things too. He's coming into his own hence I have to give Lovey thanks for this and hope that he keeps it up with his thought and values.

Lovey, well done; you've done a wonderful job in teaching him. Where I've failed, you won and this is all you. Big up yuself because you are a BIG DEAL.
Chris Martin

You are important in all that we do for you and in all that you do for me; my family.

Yes we can learn and it seems learning takes time for many of us. ***Hence woo nuh hear mus feel.***

But Lovey, with all this said, how do I stay more than true and humble to you?

I know I am true to you but how do I humble myself when it comes to you?

How do I have the right patience I need when it comes to you and others?

Ah Lovey, you're the one that knows all and I am just a bystander when it comes to you but in truth, I truly do not think so.

You are real; we just need to connect in a better way that's all.

Michelle
June 08, 2015

It's June 11, 2015 and I should have finished this book long ago. Yes I went beyond my target page but this is me when I get writing sometimes. So because of this I will include what I've omitted from this book in MY DAY – BOOK TWO if not BOOK 21 OF THE MICHELLE'S BOOK BLOG SERIES, but I highly doubt this. I will inform you if this changes. My mind is saying via Twitter but I truly don't think so.

I truly don't know because I am so getting bored of Twitter and all social media outlets that it's becoming scary.

I seek a true reclusive lifestyle for some strange reason. It's as if my mind yearns this. People and family, I truly don't know because I so want to change my home phone number. I don't know but yet I know for a fact that I could live without technology. Maybe it's because I can't keep up. No that's not it, I've never kept up with technology hence I do not have a cellular device to call my own and I truly don't need one right now either.

What if your kids need to reach you?

You ask them how they reach me.

Hate and despise cell phones period. Too much headaches I had with them so no, will not have one.

If and when it becomes vital for me to have one, then I will get one but for now, no. It's not vital hence I am more than good to go. Don't have any more headaches because I've paid off Roger's Fido.

I also wanted to talk about DEXTA DAPS in this book, but it's not going to happen. But people check out his song ***WINE FOR ME AND MISS YOU SO MUCH* with him and *BLAKKMAN*.**

Oh before I go, I have to add these into this book because they are gnawing at me literally.

Dreamt Angelina Jolie and Brad Pitt this morning as well as their daughter Shiloh. People all three were standing together. They were talking as if in an argumentative state but they weren't arguing. And to be totally honest, in the dream I thought they were acting. Thought Shiloh was doing a movie with her parents. They went off in one direction and I don't know what happened but we ended up in this place where there was fighting. All you could see was fighting. Fam and people, it was as if we were in a Sci-Fi movie in space. Star Wars comes to mind but this was not a Star Wars movie in the dream. Hence maybe these two are going to be at war real soon; hence the Star Wars get it. Hint, hint. But this is my dream and or vision so onwards I go. It was like man verses machines in my dream. Humans and machines killing humans.

Like I said, this vision and or dream reminded me of a Sci-Fi movie. The guns of choice in this dream were laser and not bullets. Everywhere we ran to was fighting. It's like I am seeing this happening and in the end this is where I got thrown into the loop. Before I was like an onlooker and or observer. In the final leg of the dream I was running behind Angelina Jolie and her brood sans Shiloh. People this women (Angelina) was running in heels. These black shoes with straps. You know them dancing shoes from the thirties to fifties. This was the shoe she had on and she was dressed in black. She took the shoes off and threw it at this ship that was chasing them. I had to say to myself in the dream really, you threw a shoe. When she did this, you could see machines. Think machines like in the Terminator movies but these machines did not have true human face and or skin. Shiny were they yes and deadly because they killed humans. Like I said, when she did this you could see machines. These machines killed humans as well as captured them. She Angelina and Brad got caught and or captured and you could see other people getting captured and killed. I did not want to get caught in the crossfire nor did I want to get captured so I played possum. Mi lay dung as if I was dead for them; the machines not to capture and kill me and I woke up out of my sleep.

Weird dream.

This is the style of the shoe expect in the dream the shoe was all black. Picture taken from the internet and no copy right infringement intended. Picture used for illustration purposes only.

As with all pictures I use from the internet in these books, I use them for reference only and if this helps the artist or company in a positive and good way, then yeah me. Well them.

Yes I dreamt about Dexta Daps but I cannot tell you the dream. I think it had to do with music but I am not totally and or one hundred percent sure. I know papers were involved hence I must talk about this man but not in this book.

Also dreamt the current queen of England and her dead mother.

Dreamt about Harry and William.

This is the dream.

Dreamt I was in this place where there were lots of factories. This one particular factory owned this building and some other places on the block. The main factory was up the street and when you walked down, they had another factory. Oh man I can't remember the name of the factory but it seems they had the monopoly on whatever they produced and or made.

Somehow I am seeing this huge dirt road before me but I can't remember if it's a part of the dream or not' so I am going to leave it alone because this dirt road is as wide as our paved road and it's clean and beautiful. No homes have you nor are there any trees. Why this image is stuck in my head I truly do not know. Maybe it's because I've seen this road before on YouTube. I am not sure if this road is in British Columbia, Canada or Alberta, Canada. But this image is in my head for some strange reason, hence interfering with my thought process and or vision; talking about this dream and or vision.

Weird people.

Like I said, this business had the monopoly it seems on what they made and or produced. Somehow I ended up going to this area and I saw an old co worker that I used to work with in my early years. Her name is Maria and she's Italian. She was making glasses – glass furniture and she was complaining about this. She said, "she does not know why people want to buy glass furniture."

A shipment of glass came in. I believe Six (6) pieces was in the crate and or package. And for you who are obsessed with 6 (six) and 666, the mark of the beast and so forth, don't come here with your bullshit. Read and when you are finished reading, do whatever you want with the six, but not now and not here. The pull is strong to come with the 666 bullshit, well not bullshit but time, but for now try to contain yourself as well as your lust for this number, the number six. Oh man stop. Do not add up the amount of time I use 6 (six) either because I know some of you will.

Like I said, 6 pieces of glass came in a package and it could be more but I am not one hundred percent sure. Two packages had two pieces of glass in each package for a total of four. At the bottom of those two packages the glass pieces were loose. So yes there was more than 6 pieces of glass. There was eight (8).

Now this is the weird part of the dream. William the brother of Harry was working in this company; he was a labourer. He's the one to remove the glass from the package. People and Fam, he had this black shoe on his feet and it looked worn; really worn and old. In the dream you could see how worn and old the shoe is to the point where the bridge, that little bridge just below your big toe; his was pushing out. Not out of the shoe but it made its mark in the shoe.

When I saw this, Harry came along in this brown suit and or outfit. He looked sharp and debonair, and he began to tell jokes. We were there laughing up a storm. He called me cous, cousin and this is where I am going to jump in. People I do not know these people in real life, nor do I know them from Adam. But every time mi dream si dem, this particular monarch dem a call mi cousin like mi an dem related. I do not know why dem affi du dis inna mi dream state, a remind mi and or a call mi cousin like mi an dem a blood; family and or blood relatives.

After we were making jokes and all, I went into this house, huge house and I saw the their great grandmother and grandmother together. We began to talk and their great grandmother was telling me how she Elizabeth liked to play tennis until this day. People and family just know that the conversation entailed tennis and Elizabeth's love of playing tennis for which she Elizabeth confirmed in the dream. Yes for me old death means new death. You have the dreams in this book and others please figure them out.

As for William and Harry, in the dream, Harry was the rich one and the more outgoing. William was more the conformer, old and boring as if he did not know what to do in life.

Oh well this is reality I guess in a nutshell.

Oh, but you should know that I am the only black person in these dreams, well this one and the Angelina Jolie one.

So as we journey along and the dreams get weirder and weirder, I hope we will find out the truth in reality.

Michelle.

OTHER BOOKS BY MICHELLE JEAN

Blackman Redemption – The Fall of Michelle Jean
Blackman Redemption – After the Fall Apology
Blackman Redemption – World Cry – Christine Lewis
Blackman Redemption
Blackman Redemption – The Rise and Fall of Jamaica
Blackman Redemption – The War of Israel
Blackman Redemption – The Way I Speak to God
Blackman Redemption – A Little Talk With Man
Blackman Redemption – The Den of Thieves
Blackman Redemption – The Death of Jamaica
Blackman Redemption – Happy Mother's Day
Blackman Redemption – The Death of Faith
Blackman Redemption – The War of Religion
Blackman Redemption – The Death of Russia
Blackman Redemption – The Truth
Blackman Redemption – Spiritual War
Blackman Redemption – The Youths
Blackman Redemption – Black Man Where Is Your God?

The New Book of Life
The New Book of Life – A Cry For The Children
The New Book of Life – Judgement
The New Book of Life – Love Bound
The New Book of Life – Me
The New Book of Life – Life

Just One of Those Days
Book Two – Just One of Those Days
Just One of Those Days – Book Three The Way I Feel
Just One of Those Days – Book Four

The Days I Am Weak
Crazy Thoughts – My Book of Sin
Broken
Ode to Mr. Dean Fraser

A Little Little Talk
A Little Little Talk – Book Two

Prayers
My Collective
A Little Talk/ A Time For Fun and Play
Simple Poems
Behind The Scars
Songs of Praise And Love

Love Bound
Love Bound – Book Two

Dedication Unto My Kids
More Talk
Saving America From A Woman's Perspective
My Collective the Other Side of Me
My Collective the Dark Side of Me
A Blessed Day
Lose To Win
My Doubtful Days – Book One

My Little Talk With God
My Little Talk With God – Book Two

A Different Mood and World – Thinking

My Nagging Day
My Nagging Day – Book Two
Friday September 13, 2013
My True Love
It Would Be You
My Day

A Little Advice – Talk
1313, 2032, 2132 – The End of Man
Tata

MICHELLE'S BOOK BLOG – BOOKS 1 – 20

My Problem Day
A Better Way
Stay – Adultery and the Weight of Sin – Cleanliness
Message

Let's Talk
Lonely Days – Foundation
A Little Talk With Jamaica – As Long As I Live
Instructions For Death
My Lonely Thoughts
My Lonely Thoughts – Book Two
My Morning Talks – Prayers With God
What A Mess
My Little Book
A Little Word With You
My First Trip of 2015
Black Mother – Mama Africa
Islamic Thought
My California Trip January 2015
My True Devotion by Michelle – Michelle Jean
My Many Questions To God
My Talk
My Talk Book Two
My Talk Book Three – The Rise of Michelle Jean
My Talk Book Four
My Talk Book Five
My Talk Book Six
My Talk Book Seven
My Talk Book Eight – My Depression
My Talk Book Nine - Death